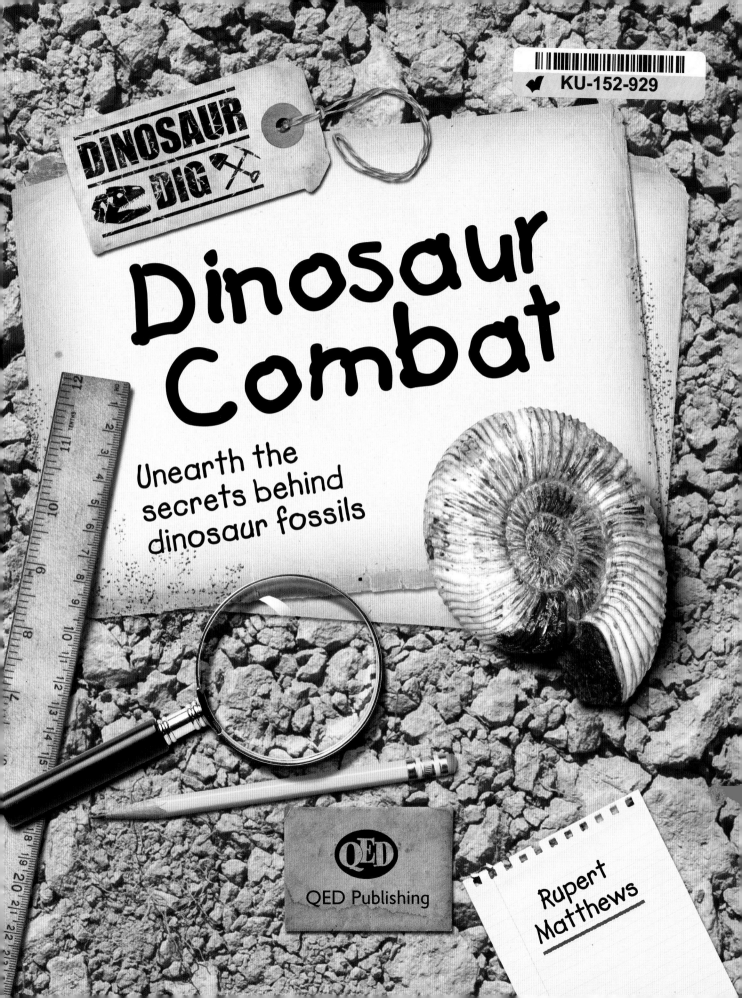

DINOSAUR DIG

Dinosaur Combat

Unearth the secrets behind dinosaur fossils

QED Publishing

Rupert Matthews

DINOSAUR DIG

Copyright © QED Publishing 2008

First published in the UK in 2008 by QED Publishing
A Quarto Group Company
226 City Road
London EC1V 2TT
www.qed-publishing.co.uk

A catalogue record for this book is available from the British Library.

ISBN 978 1 84538 933 8

Printed and bound in China

Author Rupert Matthews
Consultant Neil Clark
Editor Amanda Askew
Designer Liz Wiffen

Publisher Steve Evans
Creative Director Zeta Davies

Picture credits (t = top, b = bottom, l = left, r = right)
Corbis Louie Psihoyos 4, Louie Psihoyos 7, Richard Cummins 11, KIMIMASA MAYAMA/Reuters 12, Louie Psihoyo 14, Louie Psihoyos 17, Louie Psihoyos 18, Paul Vicente/epa 20, Louie Psihoyos 22, Louie Psihoyos 25, 26
Getty Louie Psihoyos 8
Shutterstock Bob Ainsworth 2

Words in **bold** can be found in the glossary on page 31.

CONTENTS

DINO GUIDE

For every dinosaur in this book and many more, learn how to pronounce their name, find out their length and weight, and discover what they ate.

DINOSAUR DIG

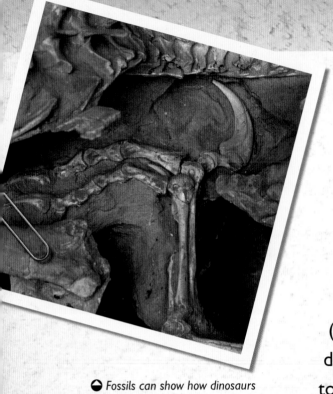

Dinosaurs **were a group of** reptiles **that lived millions of years ago. They became** extinct, **or died out, about 65 million years ago.**

Some dinosaurs were plant eaters, and others were hunters, or meat eaters. Scientists called **palaeontologists** (pay-lee-on-toll-oh-jists) look at dinosaur remains, called **fossils**, to learn about dinosaurs.

○ *Fossils can show how dinosaurs fought. This fossil shows a Velociraptor (vel-oss-ee-rap-tor) claw stuck in the body of* Protoceratops *(pro-toe-ser-ah-tops).*

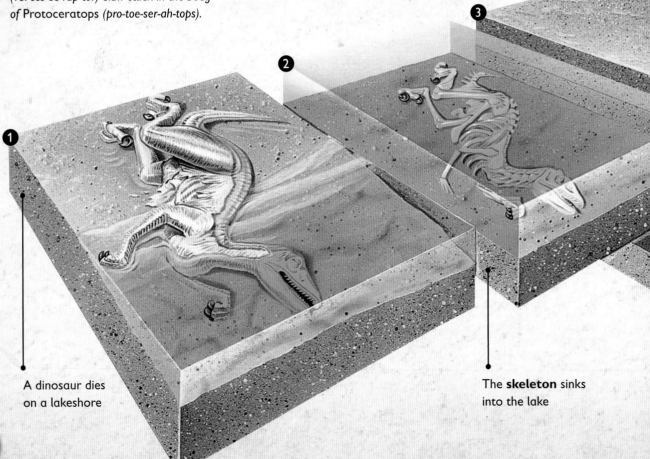

1 A dinosaur dies on a lakeshore

2

3 The **skeleton** sinks into the lake

Fossils help scientists to understand what dinosaurs looked like and how they behaved. They can even tell which dinosaurs were involved in fights, or combat, by studying their horns and teeth, or damage to their bones.

How big were dinosaurs?

Every dinosaur is compared to an average adult, about 1.6 metres in height, to show just how big they really were.

⬤ *When a plant or animal dies, it usually rots away completely. However, in special conditions, parts of it can become fossilized.*

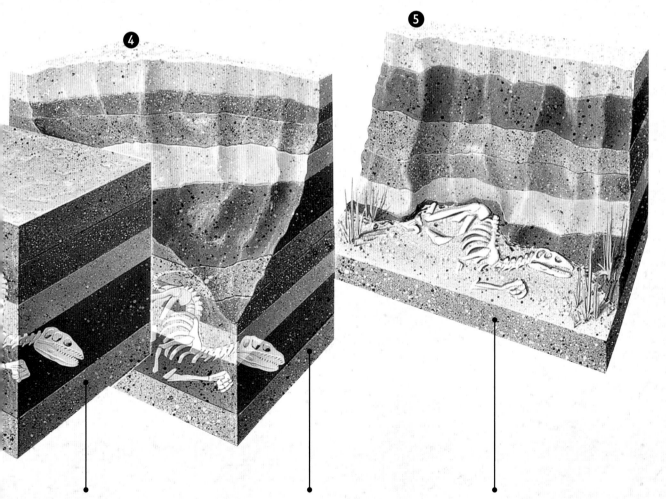

Layers of mud settle over the skeleton. The mud and bones gradually turn into stone

The rock wears away, or **erodes**

As more rock erodes, the skeleton is revealed

THE HUNTERS

Hunting dinosaurs had many different weapons for attacking their prey, such as teeth and claws.

Some hunters worked alone, but others lived in groups called **packs**. If a pack of small hunters attacked a larger hunter, the fight would be dramatic.

Herrerasaurus (he-ray-ra-saw-rus) was one of the largest hunters of the late Triassic Period. With sharp teeth, it was very ferocious. *Herrerasaurus* could catch smaller dinosaurs, such as *Eoraptor* (ee-oh-rap-tor), with a single bite. If *Eoraptor* formed a pack, they might stand a chance of survival.

DINOSAUR DIG
Eoraptor
Herrerasaurus

WHERE: Argentina, South America

PERIOD: 225 million years ago in the late Triassic

DIG SITE

◗ *A pack of Eoraptor attack a much larger Herrerasaurus. The larger dinosaur is more powerful, but a pack of smaller dinosaurs would be able to fight together.*

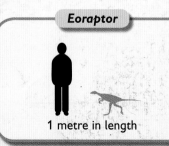

Eoraptor

1 metre in length

A fossilized **skull** of Herrerasaurus shows the curved-back teeth that helped the dinosaur to grip struggling prey.

WOW!

Fossils from the Triassic Period – the earliest time when the dinosaurs lived – show that the first dinosaurs probably lived in South America.

Herrerasaurus

3 metres in length

CARRION EATERS

Hunting dinosaurs did not always have to find and kill their prey. Sometimes they found a meal just waiting to be eaten.

A dead body, or **carcass**, that has begun to rot is called **carrion**. Some meat eaters had an extremely good sense of smell and sight to help them to find carrion. They rarely hunted at all. However, even the strongest hunters would feed on carrion if they came across it.

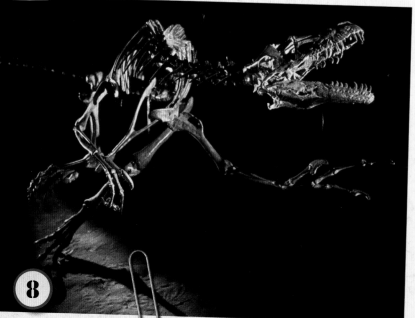

❶ *Dromaeosaurus (drom-ee-oh-saw-rus) was equipped with excellent killing weapons – fanglike teeth and very sharp claws.*

8

A group of hunters squabbles over the carcass of a rhynchosaur. Although *Dromaeosaurus* could easily catch prey, it would also feed on carrion.

WOW!

Carrion eaters need an excellent sense of smell so that they can find carcasses.

Dromaeosaurus

2 metres in length

TAIL SPIKES

Plant-eating dinosaurs needed to be able to protect themselves from hunters in order to survive.

DIG SITE

One group of dinosaurs, called **stegosaurs**, developed long, sharp spikes on their tail. *Kentrosaurus* (ken-troe-saw-rus) was a stegosaur with upright plates of bone along its back, as well as sharp spikes along its tail.

If *Kentrosaurus* faced a large hunter, such as *Allosaurus* (al-oh-saw-rus), it would easily be defeated. The only chance *Kentrosaurus* had of surviving was to hit *Allosaurus* with its tail spikes. This would injure the hunter and *Kentrosaurus* could escape.

WOW!

The bone spikes of *Kentrosaurus* would have been covered in shiny horn with extremely sharp points, making them excellent weapons.

◗ Allosaurus *attacks* Kentrosaurus. *The hunter is more than twice as large, so* Kentrosaurus *had to use all its power to escape from* Allosaurus.

 A fossil skeleton of Allosaurus shows how it might stride forwards while hunting. The head could lunge out to bite prey.

Allosaurus

12 metres in length

Kentrosaurus

5 metres in length

THE CHASE

Some smaller plant eaters relied on speed to escape from danger.

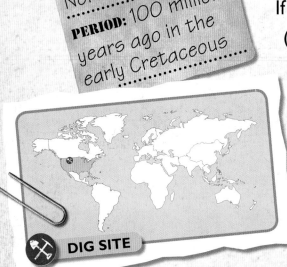

They had no weapons and were fairly weak, so they would run away as soon as they saw a hunter. However, many meat eaters were also able to run very quickly, so they would chase the smaller dinosaur.

If a plant eater, such as *Hypsilophodon* (hip-see-loff-oh-don), could run faster than a hunter, such as *Deinonychus* (die-non-ee-kuss), it would escape. If it could not, then it would fall victim and end up as a meal for the hunter.

◖ *The skull of a Deinonychus shows that its teeth were very sharp and curved backwards. This helped it to bite into the prey's flesh and hold on tightly during a struggle.*

● *If Deinonychus attacked a herd of Hypsilophodon, they would panic and spread out. One of them would be slower than the rest and would easily be injured by the sharp claws of Deinonychus.*

WOW!

It is believed that some dinosaurs could run as fast as the swiftest modern animals — up to 60 kilometres an hour.

Hypsilophodon

2.5 metres in length

Deinonychus

3 metres in length

HUNTING ALONE

A hunter working alone would have avoided attacking a large plant eater.

It would have been difficult for meat eaters, such as *Ceratosaurus* (se-rat-oh-saw-rus), to attack *Brachiosaurus* (brack-ee-oh-saw-rus) because it was so large. Although *Brachiosaurus* had no weapons, such as sharp teeth or claws, it could stamp or kick with great force. *Ceratosaurus* would need to take *Brachiosaurus* by surprise, or be very lucky, to win the combat.

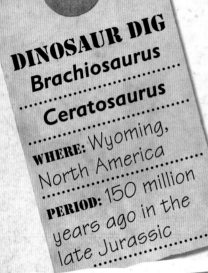

DINOSAUR DIG
Brachiosaurus
....
Ceratosaurus
....
WHERE: Wyoming, North America
....
PERIOD: 150 million years ago in the late Jurassic
....

DIG SITE

◑ *This famous skeleton of a Brachiosaurus from a museum in Berlin is the largest mounted dinosaur skeleton in the world. The fossilized skeleton had several bones missing, which were replaced with fossil bones taken from other similar dinosaurs.*

Brachiosaurus

25 metres in length

Brachiosaurus had nostrils on top of its head. This enabled the dinosaur to make a noise that may have been used to communicate with other dinosaurs.

● Ceratosaurus *prepares to attack an* **adult** Brachiosaurus. *Hunters would probably have preferred to avoid such large individuals and would attack younger animals instead.*

Ceratosaurus

6 metres in length

EASY PREY

Most hunters preferred to find an easier meal than fighting a fully grown sauropod. Young sauropods were easier to kill.

Young dinosaurs were smaller and weaker than adults, and they had less experience of how to fight or escape from danger.

Megalosaurus (meg-ah-low-saw-rus) was armed with sharp teeth in strong jaws, and had powerful claws on its feet. If it could catch a dinosaur smaller than itself, it would have an easy meal. Old or sick animals were also easier to overcome than healthy adults.

DINOSAUR DIG
Megalosaurus

WHERE: France, Europe

PERIOD: 165 million years ago in the mid Jurassic

DIG SITE

◗ Megalosaurus *prepares to eat a young sauropod that it has killed. It was the most powerful hunter in Europe during the late Jurassic Period.*

WOW!

Fossilized sauropod bones have been found covered in scratch and bite marks – probably from the teeth of hunting dinosaurs!

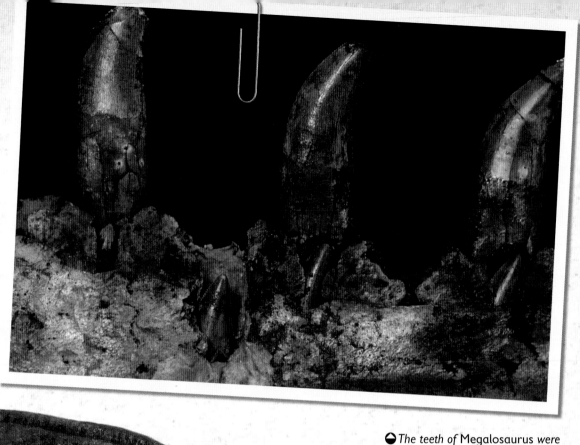

The teeth of Megalosaurus were very sharp and curved backwards. This would give the dinosaur a firm grip on struggling prey.

Megalosaurus

9 metres in length

FATAL WOUNDS

Deinonychus **(die-non-ee-kuss) belonged to a group of ferocious hunters known as raptors.**

These fast-moving hunters had a large, curved claw on each of their back legs. This weapon was held off the ground so that it stayed sharp and ready for action.

DIG SITE

◑ *A pack of* Deinonychus *attack* Tenontosaurus. *Scientists have found a fossil showing that* Tenontosaurus *had once been killed by a group of these hunters.*

◑ *This skeleton shows Deinonychus leaping forwards as though it were about to attack a victim.*

A group of *Deinonychus* may have pounced on a larger dinosaur and used their back claws to cause deep wounds. Then they would run off before *Tenontosaurus* (ten-on-toe-saw-rus) could fight back. They would probably wait for their prey to bleed to death, then move in to feast on the body.

WOW!

Some scientists believe that *Deinonychus* may have been covered in feathers, but others think that its skin was scaly.

Tenontosaurus

7 metres in length

Deinonychus

3 metres in length

THE AMBUSH

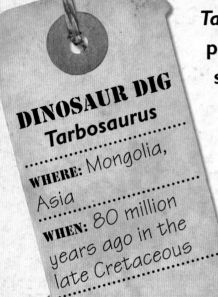

DINOSAUR DIG
Tarbosaurus

WHERE: Mongolia, Asia

WHEN: 80 million years ago in the late Cretaceous

DIG SITE

Tarbosaurus (tar-bow-saw-rus) was a large, powerful hunter. It had long, sharp teeth set in jaws that were powered by very strong muscles.

However, it was unable to run very quickly. The best chance it had of killing prey was to ambush it. *Tarbosaurus* would wait in bushes or behind trees, then leap out on a victim.

Scientists know a lot about *Tarbosaurus* because they have found many fossilized skeletons. Few other dinosaurs from Asia have been found in such numbers, so there must have been many of them around in the late Cretaceous Period.

🔴 *The teeth of* Tarbosaurus *were smaller than those of its close relative* Tyrannosaurus *(tie-rann-oh-saw-rus).*

WOW!

The tiny arms of *Tarbosaurus* were too small to reach its mouth, so scientists are not sure what they were for.

⬤ The mouth of Tarbosaurus could be opened very wide to reveal its fangs. The wide **gape** and strong jaws show that it may have killed prey by running at them with its mouth open.

Tarbosaurus

12 metres in length

WEAPONS

When a hunter attacked prey, it would try to avoid any weapons that the plant eater had. The plant eater would do its best to use those weapons to defend itself.

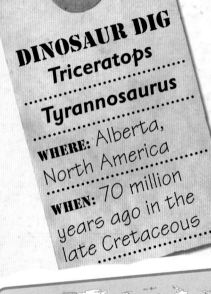

DINOSAUR DIG

Triceratops
....
Tyrannosaurus
....
WHERE: Alberta, North America
....
WHEN: 70 million years ago in the late Cretaceous
....

DIG SITE

Triceratops (try-ser-ah-tops) had three long, sharp horns on its head to defend itself against hunters. When *Tyrannosaurus* (tie-rann-oh-saw-rus) attacked, *Triceratops* would stab the hunter. If *Tyrannosaurus* became injured, then *Triceratops* would be able to escape.

◗ *A skeleton of Tyrannosaurus shows how it would lunge forwards to attack its prey.*

Tyrannosaurus

12 metres in length

If *Tyrannosaurus* could only make one good bite, it may have stood back to wait for the plant eater to become weak through loss of blood. Then it would move in to make the kill.

● *Tyrannosaurus battles with Triceratops by trying to bite into the soft sides of the plant eater while avoiding its sharp horns.*

Triceratops

9 metres in length

The armoured dinosaurs, or ankylosaurs, **had a unique way of defending themselves from attack.**

The back, sides, head and tail of *Pinacosaurus* (pin-ah-coe-saw-rus) had a thick armour of bone covered in horn. *Pinacosaurus* also had a heavy, bone tail club, which it would use to stop an attacker, such as *Tarbosaurus* (tar-bow-saw-rus), from flipping it over. A blow from the club could seriously injure a hunter.

DINOSAUR DIG

Pinacosaurus
....
Tarbosaurus
....
WHERE: Mongolia, Asia
....
WHEN: 80 million years ago in the late Cretaceous

DIG SITE

Pinacosaurus

5.5 metres in length

◗ The fossilized skeleton of an ankylosaur. Many skeletons are found with the bones scattered, so they need to be put back in position to show what the dinosaur looked like.

WOW!

Ankylosaurs have been found all over the world, except in Africa.

◒ Tarbosaurus is knocked over by a hit from the tail of Pinacosaurus. To make a successful attack, Tarbosaurus had to turn the armoured dinosaur over and attack its soft belly.

Tarbosaurus

12 metres in length

If a hunting dinosaur was extremely hungry, it may risk an attack on a plant eater that was ready to defend itself.

Tyrannosaurus (tie-rann-oh-saw-rus) was a powerful killer and may sometimes have become desperate enough to attack an equally strong victim.

Styracosaurus (sty-rak-oh-saw-rus) had a huge, sharp horn growing from its nose, which could cause a serious wound to *Tyrannosaurus*.

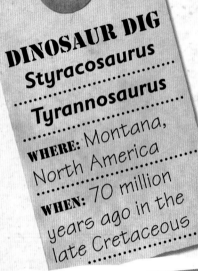

DINOSAUR DIG

Styracosaurus

Tyrannosaurus

WHERE: Montana, North America

WHEN: 70 million years ago in the late Cretaceous

DIG SITE

WOW!

One fossil of *Styracosaurus* was found covered in charcoal. This showed that it had probably died in a forest fire.

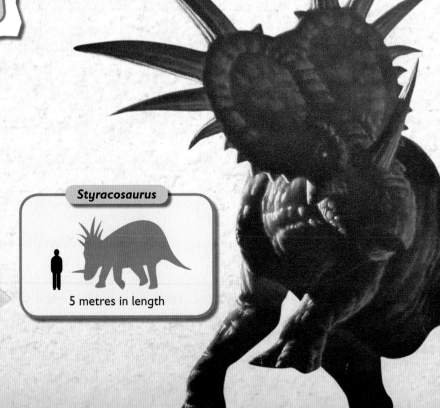

Styracosaurus

5 metres in length

◐ The teeth of Tyrannosaurus were only lightly fixed to the jaw and often broke off, so Tyrannosaurus constantly grew new teeth.

⬤ Tyrannosaurus *prepares to attack Styracosaurus. Styracosaurus had horns on its head that pointed backwards to protect its neck and back.*

Tyrannosaurus

12 metres in length

DINO GUIDE

Coelophysis

PRONUNCIATION
see-low-fye-sis
LENGTH 3 metres
WEIGHT 35 kilograms
DIET Small animals

Efraasia

PRONUNCIATION
ef-rah-see-ah
LENGTH 7 metres
WEIGHT 600 kilograms
DIET Plants

Eoraptor (p6)

PRONUNCIATION
ee-oh-rap-tor
LENGTH 1 metre
WEIGHT 3–15 kilograms
DIET Small animals

Herrerasaurus (p6)

PRONUNCIATION
he-ray-ra-saw-rus
LENGTH 3 metres
WEIGHT 200 kilograms
DIET Animals

Melanorosaurus

PRONUNCIATION
mel-an-or-oh-saw-rus
LENGTH 10 metres
WEIGHT 1 tonne
DIET Plants

Pisanosaurus

PRONUNCIATION
peez-an-oh-saw-rus
LENGTH 1 metre
WEIGHT 3 kilograms
DIET Plants

Plateosaurus

PRONUNCIATION
plat-ee-oh-saw-rus
LENGTH 8 metres
WEIGHT 1 tonne
DIET Plants

Procompsognathus

PRONUNCIATION
pro-comp-sog-nay-thus
LENGTH 1.3 metres
WEIGHT 2–3 kilograms
DIET Small animals

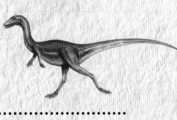

Riojasaurus

PRONUNCIATION
ree-oh-ha-saw-rus
LENGTH 10 metres
WEIGHT 1 tonne
DIET Plants

Staurikosaurus

PRONUNCIATION
store-ick-oh-saw-rus
LENGTH 2 metres
WEIGHT 30 kilograms
DIET Small animals

Allosaurus (p10)

PRONUNCIATION
al-oh-saw-rus
LENGTH 12 metres
WEIGHT 1.5–2 tonnes
DIET Animals

Haplocanthosaurus

PRONUNCIATION
hap-low-kan-thoe-saw-rus
LENGTH 22 metres
WEIGHT 20 tonnes
DIET Plants

Brachiosaurus (p14)

PRONUNCIATION
brack-ee-oh-saw-rus
LENGTH 25 metres
WEIGHT 50 tonnes
DIET Plants

Kentrosaurus (p10)

PRONUNCIATION
ken-troe-saw-rus
LENGTH 5 metres
WEIGHT 2 tonnes
DIET Plants

Camptosaurus

PRONUNCIATION
kamp-toe-saw-rus
LENGTH 6 metres
WEIGHT 1–2 tonnes
DIET Plants

Lesothosaurus

PRONUNCIATION
le-so-toe-saw-rus
LENGTH 1 metre
WEIGHT 2–3 kilograms
DIET Plants

Ceratosaurus (page 14)

PRONUNCIATION
se-rat-oh-saw-rus
LENGTH 6 metres
WEIGHT 700–850 kilograms
DIET Animals

Megalosaurus (p16)

PRONUNCIATION
meg-ah-low-saw-rus
LENGTH 9 metres
WEIGHT 1 tonne
DIET Plants

Euhelopus

PRONUNCIATION
you-hel-oh-puss
LENGTH 10–15 metres
WEIGHT 10–25 tonnes
DIET Plants

Supersaurus

PRONUNCIATION
soo-per-saw-rus
LENGTH 30–40 metres
WEIGHT 30–50 tonnes
DIET Plants

CRETACEOUS PERIOD
145 TO 65 MILLION YEARS AGO

Deinonychus (p 12 and 18)

PRONUNCIATION
die-non-ee-kuss
LENGTH 3 metres
WEIGHT 60 kilograms
DIET Small animals

Tarbosaurus (p20 and 24)

PRONUNCIATION
tar-bow-saw-rus
LENGTH 12 metres
WEIGHT 4 tonnes
DIET Large animals

Dromaeosaurus (p8)

PRONUNCIATION
drom-ee-oh-saw-rus
LENGTH 2 metres
WEIGHT 25 kilograms
DIET Animals

Tenontosaurus (p18)

PRONUNCIATION
ten-on-toe-saw-rus
LENGTH 7 metres
WEIGHT 1 tonne
DIET Plants

Hypsilophodon (p12)

PRONUNCIATION
hip-see-loff-oh-don
LENGTH 2.5 metres
WEIGHT 20–40 kilograms
DIET Plants

Triceratops (p22)

PRONUNCIATION
try-ser-ah-tops
LENGTH 9 metres
WEIGHT 5–8 tonnes
DIET Plants

Pinacosaurus (p24)

PRONUNCIATION
pin-ah-coe-saw-rus
LENGTH 5.5 metres
WEIGHT 1–2 tonnes
DIET Plants

Tyrannosaurus (p22 and 27)

PRONUNCIATION
tie-rann-oh-saw-rus
LENGTH 12 metres
WEIGHT 6 tonnes
DIET Large animals

Protoceratops (p4)

PRONUNCIATION
pro-toe-ser-ah-tops
LENGTH 2 metres
WEIGHT 150–250 kilograms
DIET Plants

Velociraptor (p4)

PRONUNCIATION
vel-oss-ee-rap-tor
LENGTH 2 metres
WEIGHT 20–30 kilograms
DIET Small animals

Styracosaurus (p26)

PRONUNCIATION
sty-rak-oh-saw-rus
LENGTH 5 metres
WEIGHT 3 tonnes
DIET Plants

GLOSSARY

Adult An animal that is fully grown.

Ankylosaur A type of dinosaur that had armour across its back and other parts of its body.

Carcass The body of a dead animal.

Carrion Meat from a dead animal that the hunter has not killed itself.

Cretaceous The third period of time in the age of the dinosaurs. The Cretaceous began about 145 million years ago and ended about 65 million years ago.

Dinosaur A type of reptile that lived millions of years ago. All dinosaurs are now extinct.

Erode To wear away.

Extinct Not existing any more. An animal is extinct when they have all died out.

Fossil Any part of a plant or animal that has been preserved in rock. Also traces of plants or animals, such as footprints.

Gape A widely opened mouth.

Jurassic The second period of time in the age of the dinosaurs. The Jurassic began about 206 million years ago and ended about 145 million years ago.

Pack A group of hunting animals.

Palaeontologist A scientist who studies ancient forms of life, including dinosaurs.

Raptor A type of dinosaur that had a very large claw on each of its back legs.

Reptile A cold-blooded animal, such as a lizard. Dinosaurs were reptiles, too.

Sauropod A type of dinosaur that had a long neck and tail. Sauropods included the largest of all dinosaurs.

Skeleton The bones in an animal's body.

Skull The bones of the head of an animal. The skull does not include the jaw, but many skulls have jaws attached.

Stegosaur A type of dinosaur that had upright plates or spikes growing from its back.

Triassic The first period of time in the age of the dinosaurs. The Triassic began about 248 million years ago and ended about 208 million years ago.

INDEX